Long Story Short

BY DENNIS O'DRISCOLL

Kist
(The Dolmen Press, 1982)

Hidden Extras
(Anvil Press Poetry
and The Dedalus Press, 1987)

DENNIS O'DRISCOLL

Long Story Short

 DEDALUS

Published in 1993
by The Dedalus Press
24 The Heath, Cypress Downs, Dublin 6W

Copyright © Dennis O'Driscoll 1993

ISBN 1 873790 47 3

The Dedalus Press receives
financial support from
An Chomhairle Ealaíon
(The Arts Council) Ireland

Published in association with
Anvil Press Poetry, London

Designed and composed by Anvil
Photoset in Bembo by Wordstream
Printed and bound in England
by Morganprint Blackheath Ltd

FOR
LES MURRAY

ACKNOWLEDGEMENTS

Acknowledgements are due to the following, where some of these poems were published or broadcast:

Dedalus Irish Poets, *Five Irish Poets* (White Pine), *Gown*, *The Irish Times*, *Irish University Review*, *New Statesman*, *The New Younger Irish Poets* (Blackstaff), *Oxford Poetry*, *The Paris Review*, *PN Review*, *The Poetry Book Society Anthology 1* (Hutchinson), *Poetry Ireland Review*, *Poetry Review*, *Quadrant*, RTE Radio and Television, *The Simon Anthology*, *The Spectator*, *The Steeple*, *The Sunday Tribune*, *Undr* and *Verse*. 'Reading Primo Levi on the Train' appeared in *Poetry* (Chicago).

In writing 'The Best Years', I was indebted to David Snodin's *Clive: A Brief Life* (Viking, 1989).

CONTENTS

COUNTRY ROADS

Black and white
marble whirls
of light and cloud
mark the end
of another November day.
Now the car
is pressing forward,
a stray cat, bright-eyed,
peering through the dark.

How desolate
the route looks
from the wind-rocked
driving seat.
On the stereo
the 'Solemn Vespers' join
with the fading horizon
to map out
the world to come.

COUPLES

The frail economies
those cars contain.

Small hatchbacks
bought on term loans.

She is pregnant
with their first.

His boss has hinted
at lay-offs.

They part with a kiss
outside her office.

Maybe his orders
will improve.

Maybe she will
be made permanent.

ALCHEMY

For so many years
I have toiled
to create
Essence of Life
as bath cubes and perfume
on a commercial basis.

But no matter
how much laughter
or even love I add
to the tear ducts and spleen,
I cannot purge
some acrid residues.

To support my children
– who eat everything sweet
they lay their hands on –
I may cut my losses soon
and sell it all off
as an insect repellent

or an anaphrodisiac.

THE DEATH OF A BEEKEEPER

On reading the novel by Lars Gustafsson

Dusk strikes early this far north.
Silver days. Then dark
no house light perforates.

I will not talk of illness.
I will take the dog out walking
to the summer huts

and know I am alive
by the swarms of breath condensing,
tracks left behind me in the snow.

Iced marsh and lake
whichever way I go . . .
I startle elks

a weekender will shoot
when this pale landscape thaws,
gives up its ghost.

Something gnaws my flesh,
like mice behind
a skirting board.

I am a healthy distance
from the hospital,
doctors homing in

on microscopic sections,
masked and gloved,
combing through my cells.

The plaster ceiling
of the sky caves in
and snow cascades,

packs my hut in styrofoam
as though for despatch
(URGENT: PERISHABLE GOODS)

to a more temperate zone.
Soft flakes, white corpuscles,
will ease my pain.

Under Alpine roofs,
the bees are stacked
in viscous sleep,

their sun god hibernates
beneath the frozen lake.
My dog no longer

recognises me by smell;
I am changed.
Snow pollinates the ground,

simplifies the shapes of things.
Then snow blots out
all record of the snow.

MISTAKEN IDENTITY

Could I begin by asking what you were thinking of as the gunman approached?

Nothing very precise, actually. I was vaguely annoyed at pet owners. It's not fair to those who walk the streets. I'm nearly sure I had a flash of memory also – something reminded me of the nest under the yew at my grand-mother's. We found a clutch of warm, fawn eggs one summer there. A woman, too, I think, a belt tied loosely round her waist?

Yes, that's right. She proved to be a key witness.

I've just recalled the way the hens would tap their legs like tuning forks, then hold their drawling notes long into the afternoon. My grandmother was always making things – knitting or crochet. Or baking. Peach flans, seed cakes, raspberry meringues.

What kind of fear did you experience as the killer was about to strike?

I was a bit behind in my work. A few times in the last month or so a pain had flared down my left thigh. Fear that the eldest would go near the quarry again, that the new video might be robbed during our holiday.

Can you describe how you felt after you learned the news?

It was a kind of reverse dream. You know how when you dream that you've done something with someone (or *to* someone, as it often is) you expect them to remember the experience too. I once flew under the waves with the kids, viewing candy-striped fish from the cockpit . . . This time, it is they who have the details; I can't remember any of it – the shot, the emulsion of blood, the surgeon, the dizzy lowering into the clay, the statement about mistaken identity.

What would you like one more sight of?

The family, of course. My record rack. A girl in tennis dress. A sky aerated with stars. Swallows in summer that pedal uphill, then freewheel down. A blackbird on my front lawn charming worms. Sparks of moonlight kindling a tree. More ordinary things – the Sunday lunch as it is served, the steaming gold of roast potatoes and chicken skin. The shirts folded after ironing. A running bath.

Any regrets?

That we are as similar in death as life, clustered here under the same headstones. But, to tell the truth, I never wanted to stand out. I would hate to have seen those newspaper reports with my name in them and the neighbours no doubt saying how quiet I was and the bishop praying for my soul and the police confirming I had no subversive connections.

Anything else you miss?

The smell of life given off by the earth that I have no nose for here. Those transparent moments at bedtime nothing had prepared me to expect. The sports results.

Finally, do you forgive your killer?

I accept death as I accepted life – as something to get on with.

IRISH CUTTINGS

I

choose your underpants
    carefully here
in tomorrow's tabloids
    you may be the hunk
of meat they show in colour
    bruised and beaten black
gashed with patches
    of dribbling red
like an ancient icon
    (in need of cleaning)
at which widows pray

II

remember the newspaper story
    of the old farmer
blown to pieces by a booby-
    trapped copy of *Playboy*
left on the roadside as a lure
    he could see her form
before him as he approached
    – the face glistens with warpaint
nipples stalk behind a silken blouse –
    an *aisling* aroused
from the strains of a Gaelic song

NOTE: 'The word *Aisling* means vision; and the vision
the poet always sees is the spirit of Ireland as a majestic
and radiant maiden' – DANIEL CORKERY

3 A.M.

I'll give him a minute longer
before I break the news.
Another minute of innocence and rest.
He is in the thicket of dreams
he will still be struggling with
as he stirs himself to take my call
wondering who in Christ's name
this could be.
        One more minute, then,
to let him sleep through what
he's just about to wake to.

COLORADO

They are crying, the sisters. It is time to part. Now they must fade back into their adult lives. Their parents turn aside, too pained to speak. Mortality is what they feel, draining their fortitude, hot tears. Where, if ever, will they meet next? The mountain air is tinged with the uncertainty of this, like white-limbed aspens brushed by wind.

And to reverse the sorrow they would have to return home, the children behaving as children again, the parents re-enacting parenthood. They would need to be conceived and born and weaned once more, taken by the hand to school.

It is life they weep for, therefore – life, distance, change – while a luggage-laden car slips down the incline, joins the traffic flow and bypasses the canyon, water cutting hard rock to the bone.

WAY OF LIFE

The longest queues.
The cheapest cuts.

The high season beaches.
The rush hour delays.

The densely populated quarters.
The comprehensive schools.

The public ward for babies.
The public house for celebration.

The special offers.
The soccer turnstiles.

When admission was reduced.
When group rates were available.

During lunchtime or weekend.
During Sunday or bank holiday.

At weddings, parks, parades.
At Christmas markets, January sales.

Wherever people gathered.
When crowds took to the streets.

FRUIT SALAD

I PEACH

There's not much point in trying
to cultivate a sultry peach of words.
Just pass me one to stroke, to eat,
or paint it from a glowing palette;
colours dart from apricot to apple,
flames licking velvet hide.
Hold its downy, yielding roundness,
fondle its lightly clothed contours,
taste its golden mean, its sweetness,
before it starts to shrink and shrivel,
starts to wrinkle like a passion fruit.

II STRAWBERRY

Strawberries with whipped cream,
a sunset ripple on your plate . . .
A cordate locket, a precious stone;
cut one and expose the marbled core.
The wholesome rubicundity of outdoors,
not the hothouse plastic of tomatoes;
compact, meaty, flecked with seeds,
the bracts a garnish (parsley on beef,
verdant ferns in a bouquet of roses).
A July day provides the ideal accompaniment,
lazy as the cream dripping from the whisk.

III PEAR

Most easily hurt of fruits,
bruising under a matt coat of skin,
smooth as bath soap inside;
halved, a perfectly stringed lute.

It hangs in a shaft of autumn light
timeless as a bronze cathedral bell
or disturbs the peace and drops
– a hand grenade, pin still intact,
a toppling shell of glycerine.
We take refuge from our troubles in its syrup,
wasps burrowing through heady pulp.

IV   APPLE

All apples lead back to that first temptation:
trees behind the thatched farmhouse,
forbidden fruit, a warts-and-all beauty,
pupating in pink silk blossom
then fired and glazed in summer,
brushed by a red admiral's wings,
wine-dipped like nectarines or green
as nettles stinging with tart knowledge.
Bite the way back to a primal silence,
your rhythmic crunch shutting out
the world, digesting its hard truths.

V   FRUIT SHOP

Orange skins baked to a crust
(fluffy whiteness underneath);
raspberries like bleeding gums;
melons whose haunches
are tested for ripeness . . .
I buy bananas racked like chops
and apricots, one blemished
with a spot (which I'll slice off,
cheddar flesh wholesome again).
I pinch a bulbous, plum-sized grape.
Lemons tumble from an opened crate.

AN URUGUAYAN BAGATELLE

On looking into a travel guide

I find it heartening to know
That, should I take flight to Montevideo,
There will be an abundance of hotels,
Salt Atlantic winds, barbecue smells.
If I care to taste the local beef
The variety of cuts will strain belief
And language: no single word like 'steak'
Does justice to the specialities they bake,
Then serve with gravy, rice or mash.
Tips are recommended (use Diners Card or cash).
This guide makes little of the open lands
Rolling from Brazil to coastal sands:
Purple prairies, countless cattle,
Sheep ranches, few Indians (their battles
Bravely lost), big cats decimated.
A beach-loving population, estimated
At three million. Roseate spoonbills on the wing,
Zorzals in the jacaranda sing . . .

Then progress to gambling and whores,
Both legal if pursued indoors.
Teatro Solís nights, the price of gems or leather,
Zum Zum disco club, when to find good weather;
The gaucho statue, parks and shopping streets,
The World Cup stadium (70,000 seats).
But nothing of crime or neighbours' fights,
Idle Sunday pastimes, rural courtship rites,
Of colonels. cloudscapes, office workers' pay,
Tupamaro threats or what the children play.
To check this book, attempt my own rebuttal,
I'd need a PLUNA jet, the airport shuttle.

Its street-map names only those avenues
With tourist promise – I'd quickly lose
My way in anonymous, dull squares:
It is like the pattern of a life, all cares
Blanked out on holiday, the pleasures stressed,
Long plain miles of tedium suppressed.

1989

Peking students on their black bikes;
shoals wavering through river-wide squares,
merging and separating in the sun,
fish that test the purity of a habitat . . .

They remind me of school-going cyclists
in my childhood, chains clenching teeth
for the final assault on Liberty Square.
(That was Thurles in the late sixties,
Mao's book colouring the thoughts
of a few red-headed pupils.)

Tiananmen Square was cleared by guns.
On Wenceslas Square, the crowds cheered
as the guard changed, bringing relief
to banned philosophers, night-watchmen,
who had waited for the light to dawn.

All was quiet on Liberty Square
in this year of revolutions,
just some lads in drunken dispute
tripping from the Chinese take-away
or my young brother and his friends
urged by a policeman to move on,
not to disturb the peace
of sleepy residents
with talk of world events.

CULT OF PERSONALITY

'Authors' photographs were removed from the covers of their books
for fear of encouraging – God forbid – a personality cult.'

– MIRCEA DINESCU

1. Elena Ceaușescu was a scientist. Learned papers
   appeared under her name. Her experiments took
   human, social, architectural forms.

2. Nicolae, her husband, was a cobbler. His collected
   works would have insulated a Bucharest apartment
   against eavesdroppers or cold. He published 17 books
   the year before he died.

3. Supplies of surplus paper were released for other
   approved publications. But their authors could not
   show their faces. The first family was not to be
   upstaged by good looks or intelligent features or ex-
   pressions betraying their country, underlined by
   hunger or anger or fear. Faces were political acts.

4. The photograph that stays in mind is of the old couple
   – anyone's grandparents – in overcoats and scarfs. He is
   hectoring the military court, flailing as if at a railway
   official who cannot make trains run on time.

5. Then the firing squad. The bodies abandoned like
   Christmas. Time to read books in heated rooms,
   authors photographed on covers (hands hide double
   chins; fingers tap typewriters that don't require the
   sanction of the police).

6. There are authors everywhere who, given the chance, would monopolise all available paper for their books; who would love the billboards at airports to display their words, the refashioned main thoroughfares to carry their names. Negative reviews are amassed like hit lists. Rave reviews are ghost-written by themselves. Writing is their power struggle.

7. Samuel Beckett shied from publicity, hated to be photographed, shunned media attention. His obituary in *The Times* was printed alongside Nicolae Ceauşescu's. Beckett's photo was the larger of the two.

TAKING LIFE

We live the given life,
follow the gossip of world news,
learn to eat stewed sheep and cows,
tilt the soup-bowl backwards,
use the rear-view mirror
to trace oncoming threats.
Whatever appetites transpire
– boiled sweets, reproduction,
race meetings – we indulge
or sacrifice to God,
our food supply sustained
by charge-card orders
or own-brand bargains
in suburban shopping malls.
We accept the hierarchies
at work, defer to the boss,
moods changeable as climate.
The revelations that occur
are taken more or less on trust,
the floods of menstrual blood,
the red nose blowing cold,
the fear of old age and taxmen,
the deliberations of the bathroom,
having adapted since birth
to illness and disappointment,
growing into the inherited rôle,
typecast by face and accent,
dressing as convention specifies
to chair a board meeting
or sign on for the dole.

Always within inches of extinction,
we see our lives through

to the bitter end.
Sunday, we read the papers,
mend a daughter's bike;
Monday, sell detergent products
or set the washer to 'long spin'.
We purge ourselves of gloom,
shake off morbid thoughts,
like the eclipsed moon
wiggling free of the stubbly
shadow of the earth,
make the best of things,
enjoy a little fame
– name in the local paper,
championship of darts or golf –
and bring up the children
to be mannerly, adaptable.
This is the life.
There is no mystery about it.
It is what we are living now,
fitting a truck horn to the car
or sitting on a bar-stool
arguing the toss with friends
or amending standing orders
through a show of hands,
our monuments all around us
– churches, prisons, flats,
buildings that scrape
the surface of the skies.

THE BEST YEARS

'I'd been through hell, being dragged to physiotherapy even
when I was feeling absolutely appalling. I'd had all kinds of
infections, my bladder still wasn't working properly, giving me
a lot of pain, my neck pain was going on, but because I was
starting to be able to move things a bit more easily than I could
before, I really did think I was on the mend, that everything was
going to be all right, that the tumour was going away, that it had
probably gone, and that I'd be walking.'

– CLIVE JERMAIN, 1965–1988

I

the misery of a common cold
        its dreariness
streaming blood–and–water eyes
        coarse throat
blocked nose running raw
        cracked voice
chapped lips, eardrums smarting
        when you blow
chill shivers make an icicle
        of the spine
dull thunder in your temples
        the heaviness before rain
drained of all ambition
        except bed
drowsing above wet
        tissue cloud
as the world sets
        beneath your snivelling contempt
(hot drinks, crisp sheets, magazines)

II

the misery of a common cold
        its dreariness
or repeated exposure to a dose
        of tiresome flu
as minor by-products
        of cancer drugs
a teenage vocabulary
        that comprehends
terms like 'radiotherapy'
        and learns
through nausea and fatigue
        precisely what they mean
and that can define
        from inside
catheter, manual evacuation
        neuralgic pain
or a slow-developing astrocytoma
        in the spine
(nibbling the stem of the brain)

III

you want to keep on breathing
        cling to life
as closely as your metal rod
        does to your spine
to filter air through
        an infection's silt
to tidy what's left
        of sweat-matted hair
still coaxing sleep
        as the discos close

(Valium crushed in ice-cream
            brings occasional relief)
to maintain belief in God, give thanks
            for twenty years
and for your writings – agonising
            though it is to type –
heaters, blankets, friends
            bombard you with warmth
(but a further cold is coming on)

BODY TIME

I

They drag you screaming
from the hot bath
of the womb
and dry your spattered hide.

II

The world you find
yourself in is less stable.
You must adjust the temperature
with gloves, lovers, smokeless fuel . . .

III

Now you wallow in a bath
that turns cool – pull the plug
and wait a dreamy minute,
water sloughing like a skin.

IV

And listen to the sound
your life makes
flowing down the waste-pipe,
the stifled noises as it drains away.

RITE

After the nausea
of chemotherapy,
after the vomit
and the sores,
bald patients rest
on pillows stuffed
with long hair
from Treblinka,
sleep off
the side-effects
of God and man.

HER

After Brecht

wasted by cancer
left for dead

flowers rooted
in her soiled body

to weigh so little
she must have taken

enormous pains

HIM

I

let me have this pair
of partly-worn shoes
so I can wear them
to the end of the journey
they were intended to complete

I will aim them
where they were meant to go
I will follow in his footsteps
before his tracks are covered over
and his route cut off

II

we bought so much ham
for funeral sandwiches

did we really think
the whole town shared our loss

the surplus meat began to stink
long before our appetites returned

III

the last bar of his soap
became a transparent ghost
and finally slipped from my grasp

MISUNDERSTANDING AND MUZAK

You are in the Super Valu supermarket
expecting to meet me at 6.15.

I am in the Extra Valu supermarket
expecting to meet you at 6.15.

Danny Boy is calling you down special-offer aisles.
Johann Strauss is waltzing me down special-offer aisles.

I weigh mushrooms and broccoli and beans.
You weigh beans and mushrooms and broccoli.

It is 6.45. No sign of you.
It is 6.45. No sign of me.

You may have had a puncture.
I may have been held up at work.

It is 6.55. You may have been murdered.
It is 6.55. I may have been flattened by a truck.

Danny Boy starts crooning all over you again.
Johann Strauss starts dancing all over me again.

Everything that's needed for our Sunday lunch
is heaped up in my trolley, your trolley.

We hope to meet somewhere, to eat it.

SPICE TRAIL

For Felicity Rosslyn and Piotr Kuhivchak

The morning is fresh and clear;
coriander sparkles with dew,

newly landed grapes are drawn
from an Air India box like roe,

flushed mangoes will be sliced
to strips of juicy flesh . . .

We have taken the Leicester spice trail
past the mosque to this saffron land

(a silk trail, too, for saris edged with gold).
Park the car, follow your nose

to the source of cinnamon and cloves,
of tamarind pods and seedy cardamom.

Lost is the England of DIY shops,
allotments, motorway embankments.

Exiled here, with tongues of fire,
we delve for Polish, English, Irish words

to match this inspired crush of flavours,
names that melt, like ghee or sweetmeats,

in our gaping mouths . . .

TERMINALS

The departure lounge:
an anatomical atlas of postures
in which friends hold their silence.

Watch how they fidget
with the coffee carton,
lean across the ashtray.

Listen as some voices reach
an artificial pitch of bonhomie.
They will end in tears.

And the other side:
salvation's gates arrived at
in a blur of wings and clouds;

purgatory when the information screen
keeps flashing *Flight Delayed*
(but eventually they come,

only slightly the worse
for their ordeal, they come
when they are given up for dead);

then hell, hell if the expected
faces fail to touch down,
scanning the crowd like radar,

and their loved ones wait –
just a few more minutes –
by *No Entry* signs.

ROADS NOT TAKEN

How tantalising they are,
those roads you glimpse
from car or train,
bisected by a crest
of grass perhaps,
keeping their
destinations quiet.

You remember a brimming
sea on the horizon
or an arch of trees
in reveries of light;
then a bend that cut
your vision off
abruptly.

Some day you must return
to find out how they end.

THE NOTEBOOK VERSION

Flicking through my notebook,
I come across 'black butterflies
in the honeycomb heart of asters'.
Too poetical, I think, too rich;
or, to cite another page,
'rich as the rain
treacling down lush leaves;
rich as summer pudding.'

Here, I jotted down
the title of a tome I'd seen:
Infections of Fetus and Newborn Infant.
Imagine landing, head first, in a place
where this text is essential . . .

Then scraps in need of inspiration's heat
to weld them into shapes –
stray sentiments such as
'There isn't much glamour
in the breadman's life'
or 'The sadness stations reek of
like disinfectant and stale smoke.'

Too much of the world
eludes the grasp of art;
there are no poems
index-linked to suffering.
And – here the notebook turns emotive –
'A day approaches when
pen, ink and alphabet
will be destroyed . . . '
Hence the endstopped cautions:

'You must write better.
Your poems have no future.
They are only as good as they are now.
This is the time they stand the test of.'

IN OFFICE

We are marching for work:
people fresh from dream bedrooms,
people whose flesh begins to slip
like old linoleum loosening on a floor,
people with head colds and lovebites,
girls startlingly immaculate,
pores probed with cleanser,
ribboned hair still wet;
people submitting their tastes and talents
to the demands of office,
the uniform grind of files.

We forego identity and drive
for the security of such places,
a foyer guard by the spotlit tapestry;
soft furnishings; a constant heat;
gossip with the copier's undulations;
crushes on new recruits; booze-ups
after back-pay from disputes . . .
We are wasting our lives
earning a living, underwriting new life,
grateful at a time of unemployment
to have jobs, hating what we do.

Work is the nightmare from which we yearn to wake,
the slow hours between tea-breaks
vetting claims, scrutinising VDUs.
We are the people at the other end
of telephone extensions when you ring,
the ones who put a good face on the firm,
responding to enquiries, parrying complaints,
the ones without the luck to have inherited
long-laned retreats, fixed-income bonds,

who yield to lunchtime temptations,
buy clothes and gadgets, keep retail spending high.

We age in the mirrors of office lavatories,
watch seeds of rain broadcast their flecks
along the screen of tinted glass, a pane
that stands between us and the freedom
which we struggle towards
and will resign ourselves to
when the clock comes round.

MIDNIGHT OIL

Sprinklings of light
in the high-rise offices.

There are mistakes
which must be rectified
before tomorrow,
awkward contracts to finalise.

More than ever now
the building is a crossword,
dark squares starting
to outnumber clues.

And, as in a room
that sends out
fluorescent signals
of a sick-bed vigil,

the struggle which takes place
is, to the pained occupant
of the swivel chair,
a matter of profit or loss

– in other words, life or death.

LOOKING FORWARD

I

We have already advanced
to the stage where we can
convene seminars on cost/yield ratio
and child sexual abuse.
We have reached the point
where genetic engineering can create
a tender, tasty, waste-free sow,
a rindless cut above the rest.
It certainly is not the experts' fault
if minds, like power supplies, break down
under the strain of our pace of life
or if bodies are stifled by the human crush
– tears like oil welling from rock –
or if hunger sears as soils erode:
remember the humblest shanty town
is still the corrugated product
of great skill and ingenuity.
Desert missile tests or rocket launches
may, on rare occasions, prove disastrous;
but we are capable of learning from mistakes
and will get things right the next time.
The alienated are just slow developers,
suffering the growing pains of evolution.
Out of the dung heap of chemical spills,
a thornless mutant rose will sprout,
its scent as fragrant as a new deodorant spray.

II

It's a great age to be alive.
Look at the girls flitting past,
styles were never more enticing,
the denier of nylon never more fine.
And watch the men, so gentle
in their linen suits, their lemon sweaters,
wheeling the baby buggy to a crèche.

Our freedom is unprecedented:
to lose faith in the church,
to choose six lottery numbers and win,
to home in close on the adult video,
weather better thanks to global warming
(naked crowds swarming to the beach
turned mole-brown on a sunny spit).

This epoch can accommodate so many tastes:
water-skiing, sado-masochism, cottage pie . . .
Lose no time in enjoying earthly goods,
for tomorrow (in a manner of speaking,
at least) we die, although drugs may yet
be found to keep us long-lasting as plastic,
durable as nuclear waste in concrete tombs.

III

'The modern order was not guaranteed by basic laws (natural selection, mechanical superiority in anatomical design), or even by lower-level generalities of ecology or evolutionary theory. The modern order is largely a product of contingency'.

— STEPHEN JAY GOULD

Chantilly lace and lycra.
Haiku and Norse sagas.
Tow bars and rotary blades.
All here by chance.

False teeth and puncture kits.
Apricot jelly and fax machines.
Laxative pills and Gregorian chant.
All here accidentally.

The stories of your life,
awkward scenes you rescreen
in the bedroom's dark
have no universal moment:

you are on your own
when long-lashed showers,
pebble-dash of hail
hammer on the glass like truth.

Only by eliminating nature,
wiping clean the slate,
will you prove your place
at evolution's peak,

. leaving pools of genes
to regroup, a cold
starlit soup on which
a skin begins to form.

ESTATES

I

This is where people live:
the rows of little houses.
Businesses have names
like Thrift Stores,
the butcher concentrates
on mince and tripe and neck;
betting shops and pubs,
drugs and bingo bring some refuge.
This is where people die:
RIP might be spray-painted
– like IRA or the big X
of love – on graveyard walls.
A lit hearse winds past waste ground;
the jew's harp of a motorcycle
vibrates from the bypass.

II

Some work themselves up
to a better estate: semis,
bungalows; show houses
with coloured bathroom suites
and kitchens where no angry
plate has shattered yet.
It takes a lifetime
to pay off a mortgage there
in potholed cul-de-sacs,
years of morning drives
through fractious traffic jams,

installing intercoms, controlling stock.
TVs, videos, music centres
drown out domestic squabbles;
all hopes focus on the young.

POULAPHOUCA RESERVOIR

'Where ivy grows on a house, the family gets worn out'
— FROM THE POULAPHOUCA SURVEY

1. The name 'Poulaphouca' means the hole of the spirit. Quernstones by the submerged cottages will be ground in the mills of God, fine as the distinction between Father, Son and Holy Spirit.

2. *The Shell Guide to Ireland* calls it 'the great lake of the Liffey hydro-electric works'.

3. Life goes on in that Atlantis. Ivy grows on houses. Haws redden in autumn. Roses are pruned back. Thatch is replenished. Bridal veils float like surf on the clear-skinned water. Turf fires blaze in the lake at sunset.

4. The Field at the Bottom of the Lane is at the bottom of the lake. The Field Under the Well is under water. A school of fish chases in The School House Field. The Coarse Little Field, The Field at the Back of the House, The Inside Field are flooded permanently. Garnaranny, Farnafowluch, Carnasillogue, Coolyemoon are spoken of in bubbles.

5. During summers of drought, you can see outlines of houses. Their owners' names linger at the tip of the lake's tongue. Chimneys poke above water like the blowholes of hunted whales.

ROSE WINDOWS

I

In the flower-drowsy deep
of a January church,
a butterfly stirs from its sleep:
a sliver of stained glass;
a rainbow unfurling
its shimmering mass.

II

The road is uphill.
Heathers, ferns.
A mica sheen.
Bracken stirrings, streams.

The train whinnies
into the distance
as you take
a tentative step.

III

Row your boat home
in the mustard dusk,
the matt lake lined
with corridors of pine.
Fish rings, shingle,
skidding waves.

IV

A bay cleansed by rain:
flotillas of herbaceous islands
sail back into view.

V

Snowdrops – milk teeth – jut.
Nipple buds suck sap.

VI

A haemorrhage of saxifrage.

VII

You wake within range of two cuckoos
– their voices bubbling through algal green –
to find creation has begun:
a blue silk-screen of hills
is printed through a mesh of haze
and everything is new
under the emblazoned sun.

VIII

An open door admits
the summery smells,
sounds of peaty streams;
hedges blossom with small bells;

thin-sliced, wing-wrapped butterflies
alight on the buddleia bush.

IX

Clouds spilling over mountain peaks,
blond streaks of surf on plunging seas.

X

A spider meshes its web
with the oil tank
granting base metal
the fretwork of lace.

XI

Just when it seemed winter
had tightened its hold

a blackbird escaped
into the cold air

bearded with twigs
like Father Time

and carrying on board
its hoard of eggs,

the songs of future
summer mornings.

XII

The tangerine cottage door,
a colour warm as a hearth fire.
Spring rakes out crocus flames.
A coal-black cat sits
by the frosted window-pane.
A scarf of smoke is tucked
inside the chimney-stack.

XIII

Gravel heaps
– purpose forgotten –
now host flowers.

Bindweed and nettle
vie for domination.
Ivy scales a telegraph pole.

It's no one's job
to curb
the blackberries.

XIV

At dusk along
a byroad,
the peppery scent
of tight whitethorn
ephemerally perfect
as you pass
in a collapsing big top

of striped light,
beams streaming
like canal water
through lock gates
of cloud.

XV

Stars mildew
    velvet skies.

XVI

Strolling beyond the cottage
on your own, breathing peat smoke,
kicking a stone, hayricks
like a tribal village . . .
Row upon row of water glazes strands:
wind-grooved waves stir life
where ochre starfish splay
and lull you with shanty rhythms
to the seabed flickerings of sleep.

XVII

A false spring
like a false armistice
brings cheering buds out.

XVIII

Lupins, wisteria, beetrooty peonies . . .
A stew of leaves and flowers.
A ratatouille of colours.

XIX

The last evening, watch
the town lights twinkle
across the bay, like notes
playing a slow air
you might entitle
The Touchstone or The Turning Tide
when you go inside to pack.

XX

Squeeze out
all the segments
of this orange day
before it disappears
into the sunset.

MAGDALA

'Young Women Face High Cancer Risk From Pill'
— NEWSPAPER HEADLINE

who lay down
        their lives for love
who swallow the host
        daily communicants
who are betrayed
        by men with crowing cocks

girls in seedy rooms
        mothers in tower blocks
lithe polished secretaries
        obeying the commands
carved in tablets of bone
        sacrificing all they have

let us atone
        this is her bleeding body
she has revealed to you
        and offered up
kneel and adore
        before you nail

your passion to her
        wide-open embrace
though you live in sin
        her grace will redeem you
skin miraculously pure
        perfume anointing your flesh

NO MAN'S LAND

when the sexes surrender
the weapons of their battle
and step arm in arm
along the precarious peace line
when they lie down together
like lion and lamb
setting enmities aside
for the sake of a natural alliance
      what words soar
      on the warm breeze
      of a whisper
      what mysteries are solved
      what promises waft
      from perfumed rooms
      what loyalties are pledged
      with lace and polished nails
      what treaties are sealed
      by tongues and teeth
      through cindery winter nights
and what pay and prospects
does the future hold
what school-to-shop trajectories of days
what anorak-and-tracksuit routines
walking a neutered dog

OPERATION

I removed slates
tight as muscle fibre,
opened a flap of skull.
There was a fungal whiff,
sprinklings of wood
like bone dust
on the vascular wires.

Fresh views had not
been aired in this
cramped space for years,
a fine grey matter smeared
the brittle beams,
dotted lines left
signs of worms.

No wonder the roof
had sagged abstractedly:
the house was brain-dead
though its heart
continued to beat
regularly as feet
clambering up the stairs.

TEMPUS FUGIT

X to III by the school clock;
a pendulum paces its cage.
Now I know what time means:
at III, I will be older by ten minutes,
this moment will have passed.

A singsong teacher lists
the industries of Wales.
The fly Glossy Gleeson freed
from a red Elastoplast tin
scales the chalky blackboard . . .

I never saw my friends again
once we had walked out
together, backwards,
through the wrought front gates
– all that remains of the school.

If we chanced to meet
what would there be to say?
What would we have in common
(crow's-feet; grey hairs landing
like some migratory birds)?

SIBLINGS UNITED

For Eithne at 21

Not a care tonight
about which of the family
is out late, sharing the roads
with reckless drivers
or who is short of money,
feeling out of sorts.
We are all here, survivors,
converging at your twenty-first.
You are no longer a child
and I am no longer required
to act as trustee
of our father's will.

United, we declare your independence.
I drink to your health
along with workmates
(you have a full-time job now,
plan a fortnight in France)
or I chat to a slim cousin
remembered with fat legs
propelling a toy scooter,
uncles last seen at a funeral.
We pose for photographs,
slip arms round waists
like life belts . . .

You cut through your name,
dripped in sugar icing
on the home-made cake,
expose the darker
layers underneath.

A close-dancing family
tonight, we celebrate
that you have come of age:
affable, happy, relaxed
in your floral party dress,
showing no after-effects
of your years of grief.

LONG STORY SHORT

A mane of grass matted the centre of the lane,
ivy vaulted famine-built stone walls.

The topiary had begun to outgrow
its own shapes, geese and lions running wild.

Flowers bloomed in Fair Isle patterns;
like Bali temples, pine trees loomed.

My steps echoed against the battlements
where a dead calf, suppurating in the heat,

was banquet for the tethered guard dog
(flews soaked in lukewarm blood).

Larval ripples surfaced on the pool
of the calf's eye, flies' static crackled.

Day held its breath, insects fizzed
in tubs of mossy water, squawk of crows.

I had walked to the pillared boathouse
when the cattle grid rattled, the barking began.

INTERVENTION

'When it comes to the EC's intervention system, truth is often stranger than fiction. There are now 800,000 tonnes of both beef and dairy produce in EC storage' – THE IRISH TIMES

Winter is bitter indoors,
colder than fields
spotless with frost.

Chopped and boxed,
frozen like sperm,
cattle are preserved,

hearts lodged
in snowdrifts of fat
(plum puddings and cream).

Marrow-clogged
plumbing connections
or sturdy beams,

bones jut through
bleeding joints,
prime cuts.

Beasts are less squalid
without four spongy stomachs
and a leather snout,

without accusing eyes
(left dotted
on the butcher's floor),

dung pouring like concrete.
Stripped to essentials,
to jigsaw pieces of meat,

the lives our intervention caused
will perish here
by lowing fridges, rustling files.

READING PRIMO LEVI ON THE TRAIN

We breach the ordered peace
of our atrocity-free mornings
forsaking the solitary confinement of sleep
for transportation by commuter train
to where labour pays debts owed
to building society and bank.

We bear food parcels
– salad rolls and fruit –
our working lunches.
A woman cradles a parcel
– slop bucket or lampshade?
Hair clings to our heads still.
Chains hang from slender necks.
So many of us to kick, to kill,
so much flesh to torture and despise
beneath the modish cuts
of suit and skirt, so many tales
to force abruptly to an end,
so many people expected home at dusk
to whisk away in cattle trucks . . .

The train clatters on.
Whatever this day holds
we will live to see it through,
march back down gravel drives,
their cindered, osteal sounds,
watch stars like gold-filled teeth
chatter with us in the cold.

REMEMBERING MARINA TSVETAYEVA

Hair straight as a witch's, face foretelling its future,
you walked these Paris streets with your chubby son
(did you starve yourself to keep him fed?).
But I still prized our months of ecstasy in Prague,
the silken skin surviving under a threadbare shift,
green eyes shining out of the darkness
where you prowled – slim and frisky as a cat –
our passion squeezed through every pore.

You were wild and volatile, an endangered species,
yielding your quivering pelt on the mountain floor.
I can hardly look your poems in the eye these days,
they hang our old emotions out like underclothes.
The Julian calendar's certainties had been abolished,
Crimean afternoons around the stewing samovar
– you used to declaim your verses then, weave your spell
Godlike as a spider in its web of entrapped flies.

The trials of repatriation summoned years ahead:
your husband would be shot, your daughter detained;
the rope you'd knot your life with would be spun.
This story is a film the audience leaves early.
They know how it will turn out; no surprises,
no reprieve, happiness never the twist your fate secretes.
What you'll learn is that the body you create and cook with
must be lumbered from sticky sick-bed to prison gates;

that love goes unrequited; that blows, like poems,
come in cycles; that truth persecutes.
Do not return to Moscow, Marina. Do not return.
Petals drip from my cherry tree, casting an arc
of blossoms, a pink splash animating spring grass

that makes me wish we could link arms again
and, among these shuttered boulevards, exchange our plans
with the surreptitious fervour of lovers or of spies.

EXPERIMENTAL ANIMALS

After Miroslav Holub

It's much cushier when it's raining rabbits
than cats and dogs. The animals for experiment
should not betray too much intelligence.
It grows unnerving to watch their actions mimic yours;
terror and horror you can empathise with.

But, for real heartbreak, take a newborn pig.
Fantastically ugly; possessing nothing
and desiring nothing except its swig of milk;
legs warping under all that weight
of uselessness, stupidity and snout.

When I must kill a piglet, I hesitate a while.
For about five or six seconds.
In the name of all the beauty of the world.
In the name of all the sadness of the world.
'What's keeping you?', someone bursts in then.

Or I burst in on myself.

JOB

What is it
that my gloomy father
gets so worked up about,
white sheets
rumpled into a lather?

And why is my mother
yielding to his whim?
And why do I
(my future cursed)
rush breathlessly to win?

Could they not have turned over
or taken more care
to leave me
in my element,
part of their gulped air?

ARBOR VITAE

I

Rooks change
the personalities of trees,
nesting in their brains:

lesions in a winter dawn
as red skies
x-ray nerves and stems.

II

The brain furrowed
with concentration, worry
is starting to unwind.

The hair shaved
for the operation
grows back posthumously.

III

I think of him at times
when my limbs tingle
with pins and needles
then go dead.

CASE STUDIES

I

It is easier to prove the existence
of leukaemia than of God

and so I pan for God
in the gold marrow of bald children

who trust in Him with passive smiles
above their Donald Duck pyjama tops,

faces magnified to corpuscles of dots
in yellowing newspaper photographs.

II

Add to the accidents
read about or known

and multiply by all the victims
named in phone-calls to expectant parents

the crushing death of this young woman
whose body was reduced to slush

as the bus she ran for registered
her minute impact with its wheels.

III

Dawn blinks into existence
like an intravenous drip.

The water trolley rattles,
constellations of beads

clouded in condensation.
Beside one bed, a draught of urine:

red vintage wine
decanted for analysis.

IV

Her chances dim under theatre lights
as she hangs on to life

by a slim surgical thread.
Past childhood rashes, teenage acne,

illnesses of old age strike home,
planted – like bulbs of ova – before birth.

A riddling which, her world
turned upside down, death solves.

THE TRAIN

She is bleeding on the quiet. When she confides in the doctor, he finds nothing much the matter and reassures her. Eventually, of course, she will be referred for tests. Meanwhile, she puts a brave face on her pain, smiles a strained smile for the Christmas photograph, keeps everything as normal for us as she can.

She leaves Thurles station for a hospital in Dublin and, looking back, freezes into a premonitory pillar of salt tears. She sees the cathedral into which she will be hauled; the schools two of her children attend; hairdressers and grocery shops. The town in all its shabby glory. A Biblical kingdom pondered from a mountain-top.

Her train eats into the landscape, passes life by.

I used to place old pennies on those tracks for wheels to flatten. They came out warped and limp like Dali clocks. As if, in the ensuing silence, time stood still.

BACK ROADS

I

soon after the Volkswagen bounces out
of Granny's cobbled yard
our father starts to say the rosary
announcing the mysteries as he drives
(the family will not stay together nonetheless)
Declan's cot straddles our grazed knees
on a back seat draped with tartan
I pretend to be asleep
a lemon slice of moon sprays its eerie light
on our seven faces (Eithne is not yet born)
he sounds the horn as we pass Tobins' house
(no point now, Jimmy and Kay are dead)
bedroom lights distinguish cottages
frost doodles on car windows outside crossroad pubs
cats' eyes and potholes, insect blizzards, sugar beet
our parents malign some relative or other
a cloud smothers the moon, all goes black
the sorrowful mysteries hover round the car

II

The road back is impassable.
I lie, a quilted astronaut, in a strange bed,
Our Lady weightless on the wall,
her head in painted clouds.

The adults natter around the range,
eating sandwiches of cooked meat
red as my uncle's weathered face,
as feast dates on his Mill Hill calendar.

I start to sleepwalk into space.
The damp-snouted pump is guarding the farm,
curved handle a tense watchdog's tail;
hens snuggle in deep-litter roosts.

I am launched into the eye of sleep.

III

My father ran the family museum.
Our first buckled shoes,
spoke-fingered men I drew,
messy attempts to write,

school essays marked with grades,
were deposited in his archive,
dated and labelled meticulously
as bell-shrine or torc.

Nothing of that booty has survived,
not a snippet of hair, not a pair
of gloves secured elastically
to the sleeves of a gaberdine coat.

He didn't even notice it was
plundered, cleared out to make space.
He had assumed another rôle,
curator of my mother's past.

The honeymoon Ford, so prominent
in the photo album, seemed
a prototype of the last car he drove,
with her memorial card laid out

beside him on the passenger seat.

IV

There are twists
on this journey
I had not expected,
unsignposted turns.
I am lost
in the landscape
of my childhood,
a muggy climate
of tonsillitis
and Sunday drives.
Every move I make
takes me to a house
or bridge or mill
that seems familiar.
Milk churns congregate
at farm gates,
men with dark caps
cycle from a match,
blue-smocked wives
begin a fry...
My dead father
starts to navigate.
In no time now
we will be home.

BREVIARY

THE POOL (Courbet)

This is the pool
without the Sunday crowds:
no one stands
between the water
and its clouds.

This is the pool
as the hill-bristling trees
and the boulders see it,
when even the painter has left.

This is the pool
as it laps itself up.

SHADOWS

Before there was no death,
then her shadow grew with mine . . .
  – KAZIMIERA ILLAKOWICZÓWNA

At first, no shadow;
only light.

It turned less bright
but I grew faster
than my shade.

Evening already:
light fades;
day ends.

My shadow extends
larger than life.

PERSEPHONE

with sweaters
striped as deckchairs
unseasonable hockey skirts
schoolgirls surprise
the winter streets
like spring

HEDGEHOG

He scoops himself into a huff
as our car-lights interrupt his journey.
I try in vain to lure him
from his bed of nails.
He strikes out with his spikes
the way that Aborigines fired spears
to deflect the test bomb's course.

WINDOW DRESSING

Suspended from the Christmas tree
in the department store's display:
black see-through nighties,
garter belts, tight basques,
flash of tactile satin,
nylon trimmed with lace and bows . . .

Should we resist this tree
as some cankerous outgrowth of Adam's dream,
the corrupted fruit of subjugation?
Or submit to such flimsy temptation
and, in the heat of the bodily moment,
combine to trace our way back

to the silken crinkle of the fig leaf?

CAFÉ

He orders puddings, sausages, bacon, chips.
He orders his childhood to be set before him.
This is his mother's cooking that he eats.
He chews and for a while is young again,
under the protection of her love.
He looks around him with lost eyes
when the plate is emptied of all but one hard rind.
Next, he will eat his way through one of her desserts.

THE EARTH

is an apple
in a mist
of sprays
dense as the haze
of burning forests.
Satellites orbit
like fruit flies
hatching spy plots,
missiles, cartoons.
Its juices taste
of sewage, nuclear waste
that seep down

to the seeds
huddled
at its core.

THE YOUNG

They are the young.
They are taking the last bus to a party.
They are having a fantastic time.
They are fancying one another.
They are drunk out of their minds.
They couldn't give a shit about the future.
They are moving to a new beat.
They have no hang-ups.
They are doing their own thing.
They have every confidence in themselves.
They are the young.
They have no intention of becoming old.

BEAUTY AND THE BAG

She holds the bag
– NECTAR BEAUTY PRODUCTS –
in perfectly manicured hands.

The small print reads:
This bag is biodegradable.
It will decompose
when buried in soil.

LINGO

when my tongue explores
my twenty-six surviving teeth
it worries at the gaps
like sores or like someone
struggling for a word
fumbling for that
twenty-seventh letter
that would free his speech

PERIODICAL

When I told you I'd seen
a Robert Hass poem called 'Happiness',
you said 'Let's move to wherever
Robert Hass lives.'

Instead, I went back for the magazine
and brought it home to you
as if I believed in happiness
as something money could buy.